THIS BOOK BELONGS TO:

Test Your Colors Here:

Even though our pages are single-sided, we recommend placing a sheet of paper behind the page you're coloring to prevent any possible bleed-through and protect the next page. Happy coloring!

Thank you for choosing our coloring book. May your days ahead be filled with vibrant colors, tranquil moments, and endless inspiration.

you set your markers aside, I'd like to kindly ask for a small favor. Would you

ving a review? Your feedback not only helps us grow but also guides fellow

oring enthusiasts in discovering the magic of Snuggly Bugglies.

Made in the USA
Las Vegas, NV
12 November 2024

11654440R00035